LIFE
SCIENCE
STORIES

Life Cycles

Angela
Royston

raintree
a Capstone company — publishers for children

Raintree is an imprint of Capstone Global Library Limited, a company incorporated in England and Wales having its registered office at 264 Banbury Road, Oxford OX2 7DY – Registered company number: 6695582

www.raintree.co.uk
myorders@raintree.co.uk

Text © Capstone Global Library Limited 2016
The moral rights of the proprietor have been asserted.

Produced for Raintree by Calcium
Edited by Sarah Eason and Harriet McGregor
Designed by Paul Myerscough and Geoff Ward
Picture research by Rachel Blount
Production by Victoria Fitzgerald
Originated by Capstone Global Library Limited © 2016
Printed and bound in China

ISBN 978 1 4747 1575 1
19 18 17 16 15
10 9 8 7 6 5 4 3 2 1

British Library Cataloguing in Publication Data
A full catalogue record for this book is available from the British Library.

Acknowledgements
We would like to thank the following for permission to reproduce photographs: Dreamstime: Noam Armonn 11, Arwyn 8, Darrin Boone 28, Emi Cristea 4, Jan Csernoch 23, D40xboy 12, Gilles Decruyenaere 15, Mark Eaton 16, Mircea Gherase 10, Derek Gordon 13, Hotshotsworldwide 27, Isselee 21, Kcmatt 7, Lunamarina 17, Andy Magee 22, Claudia Närdemann 5, Nomisg 24, Picstudio 14, Lenka Príhonská 26, Smellme 29, Ioannis Syrigos 6, Rudy Umans 25, Whiskybottle 9; Shutterstock: Background Land 19, Stefan Fierros 20, Steven Frame 18, Jens Stolt 16r.

Cover photographs reproduced with permission of: Shutterstock: Anneka.

Every effort has been made to contact copyright holders of material reproduced in this book. Any omissions will be rectified in subsequent printings if notice is given to the publisher.

All the internet addresses (URLs) given in this book were valid at the time of going to press. However, due to the dynamic nature of the internet, some addresses may have changed, or sites may have changed or ceased to exist since publication. While the author and publisher regret any inconvenience this may cause readers, no responsibility for any such changes can be accepted by either the author or the publisher.

Some words are shown in bold, **like this**. You can find out what they mean by looking in the glossary.

Contents

What is a life cycle?

A life cycle is the story of a living thing as it grows from a seed or an egg into an adult. The story begins when the seed or egg starts to grow and develops into an adult. It then creates its own young, and a new life cycle begins. The story ends when the living thing dies.

Making babies

It usually takes a female and male of the same type or **species** to make babies. Males and females have special **cells** called sex cells. A new living thing is created when a male sex cell joins with a female sex cell. This creates a **fertilized** seed or egg.

Only male deer have antlers. To make young deer, males must find a female to **mate** with.

A mule is usually smaller and tougher than a horse and faster than a donkey. It is also very patient.

True story

UNUSUAL BABIES

A mule is born when a female horse mates with a male donkey. Horses and donkeys are closely related but they are different species. It is very unusual for animals from different species to mate. If two mules mate, they will not have any babies.

Growing up fast?

How fast a new plant or animal grows is different from one **species** to another. Some insects start to **breed** when they are a just few weeks old. Whales may take up to 15 years to be ready to breed.

A helping hand

A good environment helps living things to grow strong and healthy. Plants need water and sunlight. In warm places, such as tropical rainforests, they grow all year around. Animals need food, water and warmth, too. In cooler places, they reproduce in spring and summer when the weather is warmest.

These baby geese, called goslings, have only just **hatched**. It will take three years before they are ready to have babies.

SAVING WATER

The spadefoot toad comes out of its **burrow** after heavy rain. It quickly eats enough insects to last a year!

Spadefoot toads survive in the desert where there is almost no water. They take in water through their skin. They burrow underground to keep cool and to stop water from escaping from their bodies. When it pours with rain, the toads come out of their burrows and lay eggs in the puddles.

Plants with flowers

Plants that have flowers are called flowering plants. A new flowering plant grows when a female seed is **fertilized** by a grain of male **pollen**, usually from the same **species**. This is called pollination.

Pollen on the move

Different types of flowers use different ways to spread pollen from one flower to another. Some use insects or birds, while others use water. Many, such as grasses and some trees, use the wind. They make a lot of pollen, some of which then blows onto other plants and fertilizes them.

Each of these wheat plants produces pollen that blows to other wheat plants. Wheat, rice and corn are all types of grass.

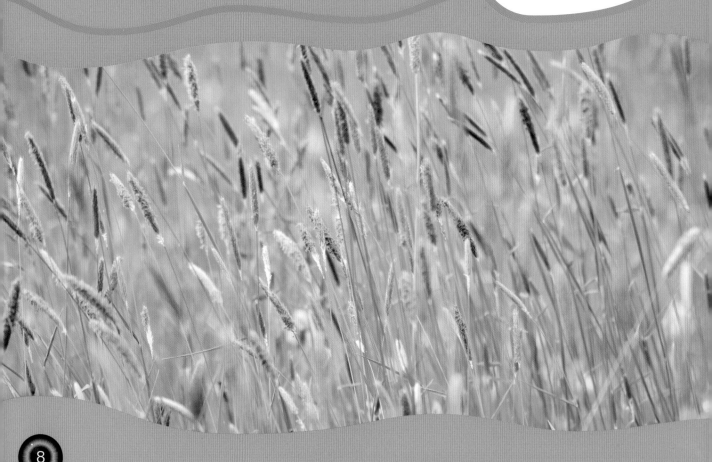

HAZEL CATKINS

Most flowers make pollen and seeds in different parts of the same flower. Hazel is different. It has separate male and female flowers. The long male flowers are called catkins. The female flowers look like red buds. Pollen from the catkins cannot **pollinate** its own female flowers. They need pollen from other catkins.

Long catkins dangle from the twigs of hazel trees. They are covered with masses of pollen grains, which are blown by the wind.

Busy bees

Many flowers need bees to bring **pollen** to their seeds. The flowers make a sweet juice called nectar, which bees love to drink. As a bee drinks the nectar, grains of pollen from the flowers stick to its body. The pollen rubs off on the next flower the bee visits.

How pollen reaches the seeds

When pollen reaches a flower some of it lands on a female part called a **pistil**. The pollen then grows a tube that reaches down through the pistil to the female seeds at the bottom. When the pollen tube reaches a seed, it **fertilizes** it. The seed then ripens.

Bees love the sweet smells and colours of flowers. The pouches on this bee's legs hold lots of pollen.

Honeybees take nectar and pollen back to the nest. They make honey from the nectar and eat the tasty pollen.

Future Story

NO MORE BEES

Many farmers and scientists are worried because large numbers of bees are dying. A disease may be killing the bees, but scientists think that the killer could be the chemicals that farmers spray on their crops. Unless the problem is fixed, bees might die out forever.

Fruits and seeds

If all the seeds of a plant fell to the ground and grew around the plant, they would crowd each other and would not grow. So, once its seeds have been **fertilized**, the plant's next job is to spread them out.

Scattering the seeds

Some plants wrap their seeds in sweet, juicy fruits and berries. Birds and other animals eat the fruit, but drop the seeds far away in their waste. Plants such as dandelions have fluffy seeds that blow away in the wind. Rivers spread the seeds of some plants, while coconuts float away in the ocean!

Squirrels love tasty nuts. They bury nuts to eat during the winter. The ones they do not eat stay in the soil and begin to grow.

Giant sequoias can live for 2,000 years! These trees grow in the Sierra Nevada mountains in the United States.

FIRE SURVIVOR

Natural fires help to spread the seeds of giant sequoia trees. The tree's trunk is so thick the fire does not damage the tree, but it burns all the other plants around it. The heat of the fire also dries the sequoia's cones. The cones open and scatter the seeds onto the cleared ground.

Insect stages

Insects go through three or four stages in their life cycles. They begin as eggs laid by a female on leaves, rotting meat or other types of food. The insect **hatches** out of the egg as a grub or a caterpillar. At this stage it is a **larva**.

Life as a larva

Adult insects and larvae look very different from each other. A larva spends most of its time eating and growing. Many larvae are eaten by birds and other animals. Those that survive carry on eating until they are ready to change into an adult insect.

When froghopper bugs have **mated**, the female lays her eggs on the roots of a plant. The larvae grow inside.

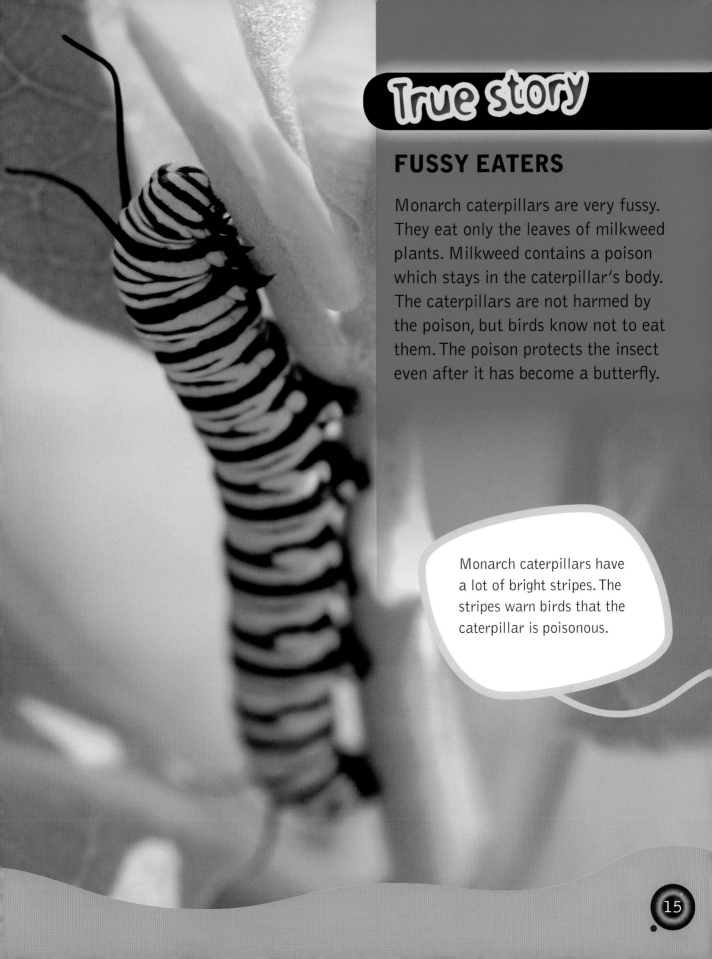

FUSSY EATERS

Monarch caterpillars are very fussy. They eat only the leaves of milkweed plants. Milkweed contains a poison which stays in the caterpillar's body. The caterpillars are not harmed by the poison, but birds know not to eat them. The poison protects the insect even after it has become a butterfly.

Monarch caterpillars have a lot of bright stripes. The stripes warn birds that the caterpillar is poisonous.

Amazing change

When a **larva** is fully grown, it changes into an adult insect. This is called **metamorphosis**. Firstly, the larva glues itself onto a twig and turns into a **pupa**. Inside the pupa, the insect's body changes.

Becoming an adult

After a few weeks or months, the adult insect breaks out of the pupa. The adult then **mates**. The female lays eggs and a new life cycle begins. Some insects, such as grasshoppers and some bugs, do not form a pupa. Instead the larva looks similar to an adult, but without wings. Eventually, the larva grows wings and becomes an adult.

This diagram shows the stages of a butterfly life cycle, from egg to adult. The life cycle of all living things ends with death.

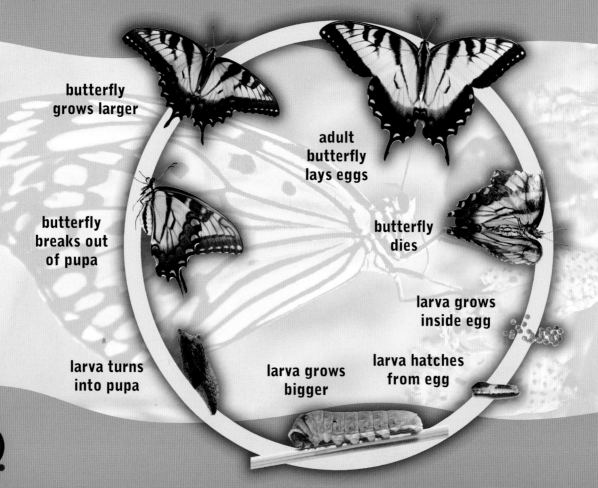

butterfly grows larger

adult butterfly lays eggs

butterfly breaks out of pupa

butterfly dies

larva grows inside egg

larva turns into pupa

larva grows bigger

larva hatches from egg

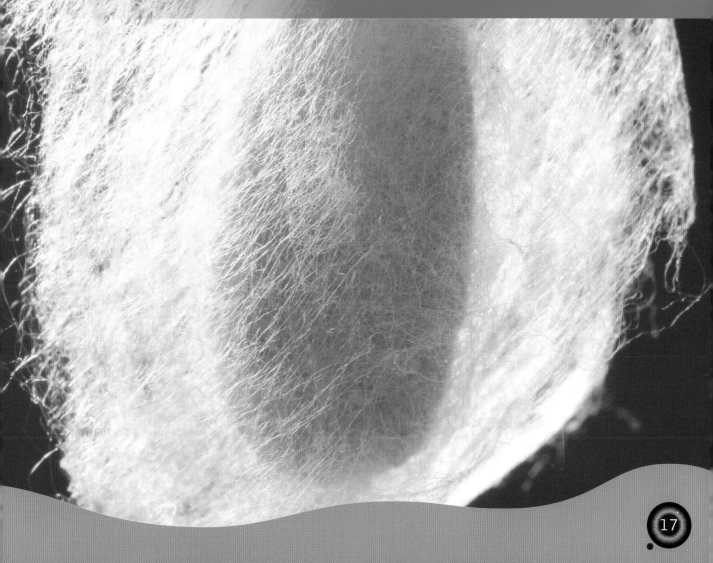

This yellow silkworm cocoon is hanging in a silk net. Each cocoon has up to 900 metres (1,000 yards) of thread.

SILK FACTORY

The caterpillars of silk moths are called silkworms. Many moth caterpillars make a cocoon around the outside of the pupa. The cocoon is made of silk. It protects the pupa as the moth grows inside it. Silk farmers unwind the cocoon and spin the silk into a thread to make cloth.

Fish life

A fish spends its whole life in water, either in the sea or in rivers or lakes. Female fish lay a lot of eggs in the water. Males then **fertilize** the eggs.

A dangerous life

Fish lay thousands of eggs, but only some of them survive to become adults. Most of them are gobbled up by fish and animals. Young fish **hatch** from the eggs that are not eaten, but most of these baby fish are eaten, too. Some fish take only a few years to become an adult. Others, such as sturgeon, take 25 years.

Some fish, such as sharks, protect their fertilized eggs in a hard case, nicknamed a mermaid's purse. These empty cases have washed onto the seashore.

Survival story

SWIMMING SALMON

Most fish live either in the sea or in fresh water, but a salmon does both. It begins life in a mountain stream and then swims down to the sea. The adult salmon returns to the stream where it was born to **breed**. To get there it swims up rivers and even jumps up low waterfalls.

Adult salmon make a long and difficult journey upriver to the stream where they hatched. After breeding, they die.

Frogs and toads

Animals that live part of their life in the water and part of it on land are called **amphibians**. Frogs and toads are amphibians. They begin life in the water as jelly and eggs called frogspawn.

Tiny tadpoles

The eggs **hatch** into tiny tadpoles. A tadpole has a long tail, which it uses for swimming. It feeds on little plants and grows bigger all the time. As it grows, the tadpole slowly turns into a frog. This is called **metamorphosis**, but it happens in a different way from insects. Firstly the gills of the tadpole close up, and then legs begin to grow.

Each black dot of this frogspawn is a tadpole. Tadpoles grow more quickly in warm water than in cold water.

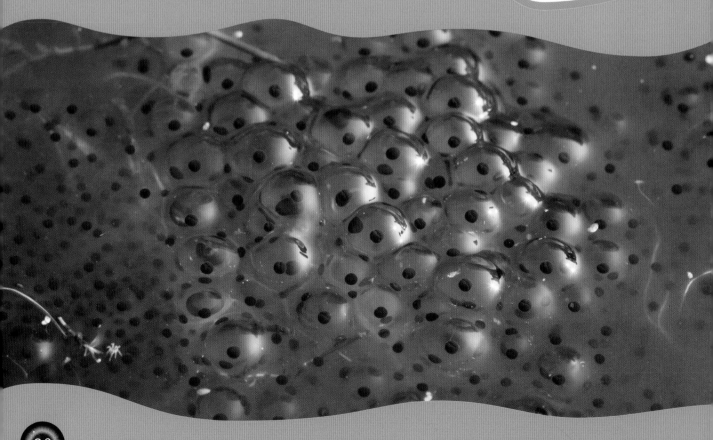

This tadpole is slowly changing into a frog. It uses its back legs and its tail to help it swim quickly.

True story

FROM TADPOLE TO FROG

When it is a few weeks old, the tadpole's back legs begin to grow. Then its front legs grow, too, and its long tail becomes shorter. The tadpole is now a froglet and it is ready to jump out of the pond. It will carry on growing for a year or more before it is ready to **breed**.

Eggs with shells

All birds and most **reptiles** lay eggs on land. The eggs are covered by a tough shell. This stops the eggs from drying out and protects them from **predators**. Birds have hard shells and reptiles have leathery shells.

Making nests, laying eggs

Most birds build a nest in which to lay their eggs. The female sits on the eggs to keep them warm while the chicks grow inside. Reptiles lay their eggs in a mound of soil on the ground and cover them with leaves or soil. Most reptiles leave their eggs to survive alone.

The killdeer bird does not build a nest with grass and twigs. Its eggs look like stones so the female lays them in a stony dip in the ground.

Female turtles crawl ashore at night to lay their eggs. They use their flippers to dig a nest for the eggs.

Survival story

FIGHT TO SURVIVE

Sand protects a sea turtle's eggs. The female sea turtle digs a nest in the sand, and then covers her eggs with more sand. When the eggs **hatch**, the baby turtles climb out of the nest. They rush down the beach and into the sea as fast as they can, before a bird or other hungry predator snaps them up.

Just hatched

Most **reptiles**, except crocodiles and some snakes, have to look after themselves from the moment they **hatch**. Birds, however, are well cared for by their parents.

New and needy

Baby birds are fairly helpless when they first hatch. Their parents bring them food and look after them until they are ready to leave the nest. Ducks and other water birds follow their mother to the water and swim when they are just a few days old. Birds that must learn to fly take longer.

Ostriches cannot fly. These ostrich chicks follow their mother until they are old enough to look after themselves.

Baby crocodiles are about 30 centimetres (1 foot) long when they hatch. They take more than 10 years to grow as big as their mother.

True story

LOOKING AFTER BABIES

A female crocodile looks after its eggs and the babies when they hatch. It stays close to the nest and chases away **predators**. When the babies hatch, the mother carries them to the water in her mouth. The mother looks after the babies for weeks or years.

Mammals and babies

Cats, dogs and most other **mammals**, including humans, give birth to babies. The **fertilized** egg develops inside the mother's body. When the baby is born, the mother feeds it with her milk.

How many babies?

Humans and other large mammals usually have one or two babies at a time. Smaller mammals, such as cats, mice and rabbits, have a **litter** of several babies. As well as feeding her babies, the mother cleans them and teaches them the skills they will need to survive on their own.

This litter of kittens snuggles up close to the mother. These kittens are quite big and will soon leave her and look after themselves.

Koalas live in eucalyptus trees. This koala's baby joey is big enough to leave the pouch. It clings on to its mother's fur.

True story

KEEP ON GROWING

Animals called **marsupials** give birth to babies that are not fully formed. Their babies are called joeys. A koala is a marsupial. Its joey is born with no ears or fur. It crawls into a pouch on its mother's belly, where it drinks her milk and keeps on growing.

Growing up

Some **mammals** take longer than others to grow into adults. Mammals that live only a year or two, such as mice, grow up quickly. Mammals that live for many years, such as elephants, take longer to grow up.

A lot to learn

Intelligent **species** take longer to grow up. They have a lot to learn before they can fend for themselves. Lions learn to fight and to hunt. Humans have to learn almost everything, including walking and talking. When they are grown up, they will begin another life cycle by having babies of their own.

This **litter** of young mice will stay in the nest for around three weeks. They will start to **breed** when they are around five weeks old.

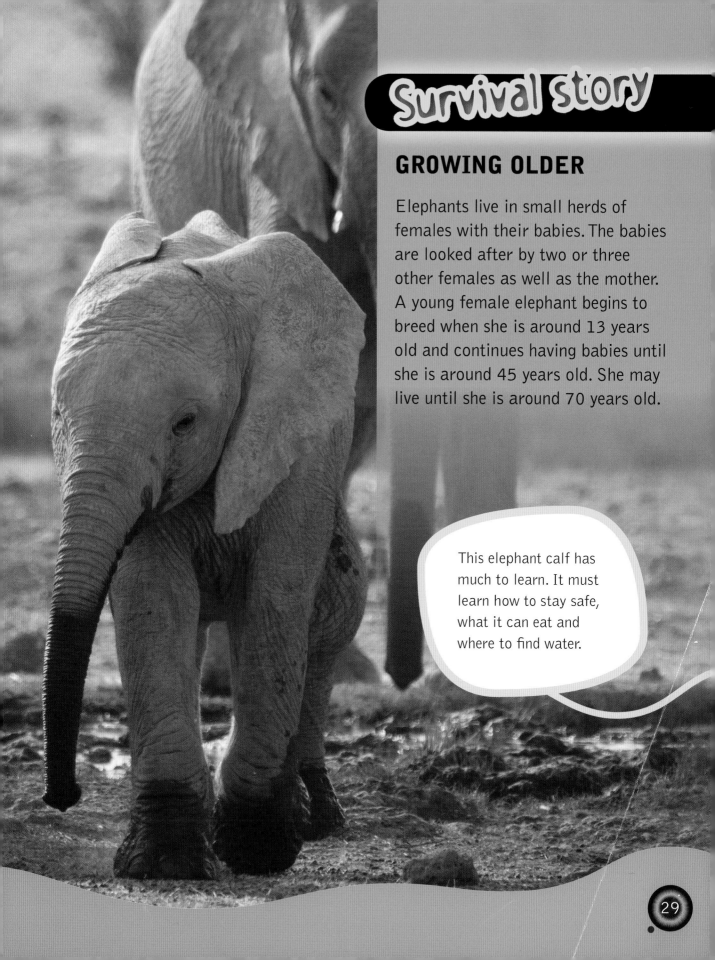

GROWING OLDER

Elephants live in small herds of females with their babies. The babies are looked after by two or three other females as well as the mother. A young female elephant begins to breed when she is around 13 years old and continues having babies until she is around 45 years old. She may live until she is around 70 years old.

This elephant calf has much to learn. It must learn how to stay safe, what it can eat and where to find water.

Glossary

amphibian animal that begins life in water but changes as
  it grows so that it can also live on land

breed mate with another animal of the opposite sex

burrow hole underground in which an animal lives

cell small unit from which living things are made

fertilize when a female egg joins with a male sex cell
  and is able to develop into a new individual

hatched broken out of a shell

larva early stage of an insect's life after it has hatched

litter group of animals born to the same mother at one time

mammal animal that feeds its young with milk

marsupial animal whose baby lives in a pouch while it grows

mate when a male and a female come together to have babies

metamorphosis change that insects and amphibians go
  through to become an adult

pistil part of a flower where seeds grow

pollen male sex cells of a plant

pollinate carry pollen from one flower to another

predator animal that hunts and eats other animals

pupa stage in which an insect changes from a larva into an adult

reptile animal that is covered with dry, scaly skin. A reptile
  is cold-blooded and must take in heat from around itself.

species group of animals that are so alike they can produce young

Find out more

Books

Bugs and Spiders (Amazing Life Cycles), George C. McGavin (TickTock Books, 2014)

Ocean (Life Cycles), Sean Callery (Kingfisher Books, 2012)

The Life Cycle of Mammals (Life Cycles), Susan H. Gray (Raintree, 2011)

Websites

www.childrensuniversity.manchester.ac.uk/interactives/science/ microorganisms/mushroomlifecycle
Follow this interactive story to find out all about how mushrooms reproduce.

www.ngkids.co.uk/did-you-know/butterfly-life-cycle
Visit the National Geographic Kids website for fascinating facts about the butterfly's life cycle.

www.oum.ox.ac.uk/thezone/animals/life/produce.htm
Uncover the secrets of the human life cycle.

Index